A new an upcoming Author AriQui is here to tell it like it is. A single mother of two handsome young men Jeremiah Taylor and Matthias McGee.

AriQui's message is that without quality communication relationships, regardless (if you are married, single, dating, or just friends), will struggle and many times fail. Through her writing she hopes to bring about healing, understanding and the importance of how we should and need to effectively communicate with one another.

JUST TALK TO ME

Q

Just talk to me is available for bulk purchasing. For details please contact the author Arica Quinn directly at ariquibooks@gmail.com or at (276) 624-7844.

Just Talk To Me
Published By Cenece Dixon Publishing
P.O. Box: 32023 Aurora CO 80041
515-992-6657

Cover Design By Dante Toms, dante.toms@yahoo.com
Author Photos: Kymora Jaxson Photography,
www.kymorajacksonphotography.com

Library of Congress Cataloging-in-publication Data
2014955412

ISBN 978-0-9909429-0-0

Printed in the US

Dedication

To myself, my friends, and to your friends. To every person man or woman who wishes someone would just talk to them. Whether it's a husband and wife, boyfriend and girlfriend, parent and child, friend to friend.
Communication is key in any relationship and is vital to the success of that relationship. So I dedicate this book to all of us who have been hurt, mistreated, abused and rejected through inadequate communication. I hope you experience healing through each page of this book as you read it just as I did through writing it.

Contents

Acknowledgment

I want to thank some very special and dynamic people, whom without them my dream to bring Just Talk To Me to the world would not have been realized. I thank each of you for your support, friendship and commitment.

1.   Seven Sevante: Without your push to write I never would have picked up the pen and pad in the first place.

2. Yvonne McCoy (mom): For being there to talk to through my failed relationships and for taking time to read my story and write a wonderful, well thought out Introduction.

Contact Information:
His Healing Hands
Po Box 441064
Aurora, CO 80014
hhhands1@gmail.com, hhhands.net
(951) 444-1833

3. My Children (Jeremiah Taylor and Matthias McGee): For putting up with me when I was in my writing zone and giving me the space and time to write.

4. Cenece Dixon Publishing: For understanding the vision and opening the door for this book to be available to the world.

5. Dante Toms (Graphic Designer): For the most incredible book cover design. You truly captured the essence of the book and the message I desire to convey.

6. Kymora Jaxson Photography: Hands down the best studio ever. You truly brought out the real me that has been hidden for far to long. You embodied my concept for the inside cover and, through your lens, brought it to life.

Contact Information:
Zsa'nee Gaines, Lead Photographer
303 Airport Blvd. Suite 110, Aurora, CO 80011
kymorajaxsonphotography.com
info@kymorajaxson.com
720-295-8557

7. Zimtek Studios/Fresh Records DBA Spiritually Fresh Entertainment for taking my audio book vision and giving it a voice and a platform to grow, develop and mature.

Contact Information
Zimmeri McNeal
2550 S Colorado Blvd. Denver, CO 80222
zimtekstudios.com
contactus@zimtekstudios.com
720-550-6121

INTRODUCTION

Romance can be so unpredictable with its ups and downs. The challenges can be so overwhelming. But the outcomes of can also be so intriguing. "Just Talk To Me" will take you through the lives of several couples whose relationships have been uncertain to say the least. The circumstances of their lives and the outcomes will cause you desire to see them resolve their issues and truly love. Their incompatibility, lies and lack of trust have woven these lives together through friendship and pain.

Communication and trust are so important in a relationship. But as you glaze through this story you will see the imperfection, yet the beauty in each character as their lives are reformed and transformed. The suspense of each couple's escapades will keep you longing for more.

"Just Talk To Me" is worth every bit of your time. Take a moment to engage and see which one of the characters may really turn out to be you. This is a classy tale of love, rejection and forgiveness. You will be captivated as you stroll through the pages and see that life can and often will be a mystery.

JUST TALK TO ME

An AriQui Novella Series

The language of this book was purposefully
written in everyday "real talk" conversation. Be aware: it is
intentionally that it is **_NOT_** grammatically correct .

As the alarm blares and the blinds open, allowing subtle rays of light to shine through, Maxwell swings his long, dark chocolate legs to the side of the bed. With his head resting in his hands, "Man, another day. God let this be a day with no nonsense."

Standing and stretching his thick, muscular broad shoulders to get the kinks out, he walks to the bathroom and starts his shower.

Across town Myra stands in the kitchen in her purple robe, sipping a freshly brewed cup of coffee. Opening the almost empty fridge, she wonders out loud, "What do I feed these boys for breakfast? They had eggs and bacon yesterday, maybe pancakes and sausage."

Just as she closes the refrigerator door, she is greeted by a warm hug around her legs.

"Good morning, Momma."

"Good morning, baby, Is your brother up?"

"I thinks so, I go see."

Watching her five-year-old run down the hall yelling at the top of his lungs, "Bo Bo," a soft smile graces her warm mocha face.

***

Out of the shower and dressed in his light grey pinstriped suit, light blue shirt and navy paisley tie, Maxwell walks into the kitchen, pours a tall, cold glass of orange juice, and answers his iPhone.

"Hello, hey Keith. Yeah, I'll be there in about ten minutes, peace." Maxwell downs his orange juice then grabs his briefcase, jacket and keys.

As he locks his door, Kiki from down the hall says, "Good morning," while waiting for the elevator.

"Hey, Kiki how are you?"

"I'm good, Max. How was your evening?"

"It was fine, nothing special," he says as the elevator door opens to the lobby. "I'll talk to you later, Kiki."

Watching him stride out the front doors, she thinks, *Ooh wee, I want that man.*

***

"All right, boys, let's go. You're going to be late for school; Chop, chop."

"Okay, Momma, here we come."

Getting in the car, Myra reminds them to put on

their seat belts. Pulling out of the complex, Myra watches the cars go by, day dreaming of the day she will have her dream car.

"Momma, snap out of it. You can go."

Merging into traffic, she says, "Are you ready for your finals today, Immanuel?"

"I'm ready. I am so glad summer vacation and graduation are almost here."

"Me, too," says Nathan.

***

Pulling up to Keith's house, Maxwell blows the horn. Rolling down his window, he honks again. Finally Keith emerges, six feet four, sun-kissed brown skin, dark brown eyes and L.L Cool J lips.

As he gets in the car, Maxwell asks, "So, Keith, what's up with your car?"

"It should be out of the shop on Friday. Man, Max, I can't believe it she caused $1,800 worth of damage."

"I told you to watch out for her, man."

"I know, Max, but I didn't even do anything. I'm still trying to figure out why this happened."

***

Walking into the salon, Myra opens the blinds, turns on the open sign, and starts the coffee. "I hope these clients are on time today."

The door opens and in walks Angelina, five feet eight, smooth caramel complexion, long, straight, silky hair cascading down her back and hazel green eyes.

"Myra girl, how are you and the boys today?"

"I'm good and the kings are fine."

"Myra, do these jeans look okay on me?"

"Angelina please, you know you look hot with your little self. Unlike me with all the astronomical force I carry around." They laugh.

***

Maxwell Thaddeus Anderson, quite the eye candy, is thirty-six, an attorney, and single. Graduated from Howard University, he is on his way to being partner at Rowan, McEwen and Stein, a top-notch law firm in West Palm Beach, Florida.

"Mr. Anderson, Ms. Monique Johnston is here to see you," his executive administrator Kim announces over the intercom.

"Tell her I will be right out. Opening the office door, Ms. Johnston, please come in. Monique why did you do that to Keith's car?"

" What? Maxwell, you know he had it coming."

" Okay but to key a brother's car like that, and cause $1800 of damage."

"Well, at least he will think about his actions next go around. Any who, I wanted to know how things were going with my legal matter."

"Well, Monique, it looks like things are in your favor, but let's not get ahead of ourselves."

"Okay, Maxwell, but how much longer before we know something?"

"Probably about another month. There is a lot of red tape to cut through."

"Well, thank you for your time."

"Just see Kim on your way out and she will set the next appointment. And be nice to Keith."

"Yeah, yeah, Whatever."

Back at the salon, it's busy as usual. However it should be, considering Le'Reauxs is the top salon and spa in the Miami area. Everyone who is anyone makes an appointment here: television stars, movie stars, sport figures, politicians, in addition to everyday folks.

There is a section for the little ones with plasma TV's at each station and wireless ear plugs so each child can watch the movie of their choice as they sit in a plush Disney character chair.

Then, there is the teen section stocked with PlayStation 3, Xbox Kinect, Wii, pool table, air hockey and foosball.

For the grown folks, there is good music, soft leather chairs and everything you can think of that is pampering, whether you are a man or a woman. Oh, and did I fail to mention the one-of-a-kind juice bar and café?

With an establishment like this, it is hard to understand why Myra doesn't have the things she wants for herself and her boys. But then to know why, you would have to go back a few years, a place she does not like to venture.

It's Friday so that means her girls, *the girl Friday crew* as she calls them, will be in to have their hair and nails done. Just like clockwork Monique and

Kiki arrive at two.

"All right, ladies, so what spot are yawl going to tonight?"

"Well, that depends if you are going with us," Kiki chimes in. And don't be giving us that, 'I can't because of the boys' excuse. Angelina's daughter already said she would watch Nathan and Immanuel is already gone to hang with his boys. So what's up, girl? You coming or not?

"All right, Club Nazi, I'm coming."

"Good, then why don't we make it a glam night?"

***

It's five in the evening when Keith knocks on Maxwell's office door. Peeking his head in, he asks, "Man, you ready?"

"Give me 10 more minutes to wrap up this deposition and I will be."

"All right. I talked with the fellas and they are down for taking a ride to Miami tonight."

"Okay, man, let me finish and we can get out of here."

Miami! Wow I haven't been there since I was with... Snap out of it, Max! You said you were over that, and you are over it, right? Focus on what you are doing so you can get out of here.

"Keith," Max says over the intercom, "let's go."

Getting in the car, he asks, "So what spot are we going to?"

"We decided to wait to we get to the Ami and see what happens."

"I'm down for any place except…"

"Oh, come on Max, really says Keith. Don't tell me you still can't go there. It's been two years now and she still got you tied up like that! When you gonna face the demon, man? So what if she's there, at least you can see her, get over it and move the hell on."

***

Glam night? Why glam night? They know I have nothing to wear. Look at me. Damn, everything I put on looks awful. If I didn't have all this stomach and behind, I might be able to find something. Ugh! I disgust myself. Forget it. I'm not going. What man is ever going to want to talk to me!

Tears are streaming down Myra's face when the doorbell rings. "Who is it?" she asks glumly as she tries to wipe her face.

"It's Angelina, girl."

Great, just who I need to see right now with her beautiful self. Myra opens the door.

"Girl, are you all right? What's wrong and why aren't you ready?"

"I'm not going, but you go and have a good time."

Looking at Myra's face, Angelina can tell she has been crying.

"Myra, I am not going to let you sit in this house and wallow. Come on, girl, let's go make you stunning."

"Stunning. Me? Yeah, right, Angelina. Look at me. Nothing about me says stunning."

Angelina thinks to herself, *Damn, I told them not to do glam night.*

"Baby, come on, I got you. When I am done, you will see just how stunning you are."

***

Pulling away in his brand new, white Tesla Model

S, Max yells, "All right, man, I'll be back in a couple of hours to pick you up. And Keith, be ready."

"I will," Keith yells back as he goes inside.

Miami. What the hell am I thinking, going to Miami? That place has nothing but bad memories. Jasmine was so perfect, or so I thought until I found her two days before our wedding with Anthony. My girl and my brother. Isn't that some....I haven't been to Miami since then.

What do I do if I see her, see them, since they are married now? Why did I even agree to this? What the hell was I thinking? Maybe I can skip out tonight.

Okay, Maxwell, I guess this is it, time to face the demons as Keith put it. Stop tripping, you probably won't even see them. But what if I do? Then what? I guess I'll cross that bridge when I get there. Who knows, this may be the night a true queen comes into view.

***

Grateful, with tears in her eyes, Myra says, "Angelina, wow. I never thought I could look like... I mean, wow, really."

Angelina hugs her. "Girl, you *are* hot. In a quote

from my favorite movie, you are PHAT– pretty, hot and thick. You look like a queen."

" You and your Phat Girls' movie quotes." They share a good healthy laugh.

"Okay, let's go. I can't wait to see Kiki's and Monique's faces when they see you. Shoot, I might even need to go home and change now."

Taking one last look in the mirror, Myra thinks, *Damn, girl, you really look stunning. Hmm, wonder if this night a king might finally spot you.* "I'm ready."

***

Keith better be ready. I'm already not wanting to take this ride. Maxwell honks the horn and Keith comes right out. *Damn, I was hoping he wouldn't.*

"Well, maybe we ought to call you Max-a-million tonight. You should have called a brother and told him you were going to step out like that."

"Whatever. So, are we picking up the fellas or are we meeting them at the usual Miami dinner spot first?"

"We are meeting them."

Good, he sighed. *That way if I want to bounce*

early I can, and Keith can ride back with them.

"Oh, man, Max, I almost forgot to tell you about the call I got about 20 minutes ago."

"What call was that?"

"It was Monique," Keith said, looking at him,shock on his face.

"Monique! What? Are you kidding me?"

"Nah, man."

"What she say?"

"Not tonight, man. We'll talk later."

"Cool."

Max hits the button on the remote to play some old school. They ride out to the sounds of the O'Jays, Whispers and Ohio Players.

***

"Myra, you look amazing, girl!" Monique exclaims as she spins her around.

"You do," Kiki agrees.

Angelina smiles. "Okay, ladies, let's do this." They pull up to the Bianca at Delano and Angelina hands the keys to the valet. Hooking arms, they strut into the restaurant.

"We have a reservation for four under Le'Reaux."

"Right this way, ladies," the maitre'd responds.

The restaurant is five-star with a stylish and sophisticated interior design.

"Oh no," Monique says, in shock.

"What, girl? What's wrong? You look like you seen a ghost," Angelina responds.

" I don't believe it. Keith is here," she answers motioning in his direction. Just then, Keith looks up and meets the unsettling gaze in her eyes. A knot quickly forms in the pit of her stomach.

He quickly drops eye contact, mumbling "Damn, she looks good."

"What was that? Who looks good?"

"Nothing, man. Nothing," Keith replies to Thomas's question.

"Oh," interjects Jonathan. "I see the problem. It's Monique."

"Keith, man," Maxwell queries, not meaning to deny his friend's state of shock, "who is that goddess walking in with her?"

"I… who, which one are you referring to?"

"Her," Maxwell points as Myra enters the room, 5 feet 5, about 273 pounds, stacked and thick in all the right places. She is wearing a black and red African wrap-around dress with matching head wrap, oversized earrings and heels to accentuate the shape of her thick beautiful legs.

"I don't know who she is, Max. I've never seen her before."

"So why don't you go speak to Monique and find out?"

"Are you crazy? I am NOT going to that table!"

"Whatever, you chicken."

At the club following a wonderful dinner, the ladies scan the room for those they consider to be worthy of a dance or two. Angelina spots a cutie from across the room and excuses herself to make her move. The other ladies sit at the table, sipping on their drinks, talking and enjoying the music.

"I'll be back," says Monique. "I need to go to the restroom." She leaves the table.

Soon after, a nice looking brother walks over to

the table and asks Kiki to dance. Taking his hand and smiling, Kiki looks back at Myra and waving.

Well, Myra thinks to herself, *another night of dancing by myself as usual. No big, I'm so used to it now that I have a good time all by myself.*

She eyes a spot on the dance floor and proceeds to gravitate in its direction. Once on the floor, Myra does her thing, moving and grooving to the music. After dancing a few songs, she returns the table to find Monique.

"Girl, why aren't you dancing?" she asks.

"I'm not in the mood, I guess."

"Does this have anything to do with Keith being at the restaurant?" "

"I don't know Myra. I just felt something when I saw him, something I don't know how to explain."

"Monique, you still love him, don't you?"

"I don't know. I mean, I guess… Okay, yes dammit! So what do I do? After everything I put him through, why in the world would he want to bother with me a second time?"

"Look, girl, if you still feel that way, stop being

difficult and talk to the man. I am sure he is not over you either, and the both of you know you belong together. I've never seen two people be so bull-headed. He told you from the beginning of the situation he would be there for you and you just pushed him away because you just have to be an independent woman. Damn, girl, you got it good and don't even know it. Why is it when a sister gets a good one, she runs him off for a no good one?"

"Damn, Myra."

"Sorry, girl. I just hate to see you miss out on your king. One of us has got to get one." They laugh and give each other a hug.

Just then, Kiki comes back to the table. "Dang y'all, that fine ass man and his boys just walked in."

"What man?" asks Monique.

Pointing towards the door, "That fine man," Kiki answers. Standing at the door is Maxwell, Keith, Thomas and Jonathan.

"Well Monique, this must be your night," Myra says glancing at Maxwell. At 6 feet 6, his 210 pounds body with less than six percent body fat. He had soft, smooth, dark double- dipped chocolate skin, was slightly bow-legged, with nice arms, chest and an obvious six-pack. He had short wavy hair and his ears were pierced.

"Damn, he sure is fine."

While the ladies sat at their table sipping on martinis, and after some persuasive intervention from his boys, Keith walks up to the table.

"Hello, ladies. Hello, Monique."

Looking up at Keith from the corner of her eye, Monique acknowledge, "Hi, Keith."

"Excuse me for being rude. I am Keith and you are?"

"I'm Myra. Pleased to *finally* meet you, Keith," she says, giving a subtle grin to Monique.

"Monique," Keith whispers as he extends his hand, "would you like to dance?"

After a slight hesitation, she places her hand in his and nods. Feeling his touch, a warmth shoots through her body. She closes her eyes for a split second to reminisce. When she glances back at the table, her girls give her thumbs up. Monique squeezes Keith's hand a little tighter. He looks down at her and smiles.

***

Early in the morning, Myra is awakened by her son Immanuel.

"Mama, Mama, you all right? Wake up!"

Startled from her sleep and opening her eyes to see a man's face, not realizing it's her son's, she screams.

"Mama," Immanuel says, "It's me, Mama."

Grabbing his mother in his arms, he rocks her as she weeps.

"Mama, you still have those nightmares?"

She nods her head and buries her face in her 17 year old son chest. He whispers, "I knew I should have killed him when I had the chance.

In his office sipping on a hot cup of coffee, Maxwell is reading over his deposition when his mind drifts back to July 7, 2007.

"The 7th month, the 7th day, of the 7th year," he mumbles. *I thought seven was supposed to be a lucky number.*

That day he was supposed to be standing in front of the church, waiting for the love of his life to walk down the aisle. Instead he found himself in a hotel room in the dark, drunk out of his mind, contemplating suicide or murder.

He snapped back to reality at Kim's voice over the speaker, "Mr. Anderson, there's a Jasmine here to see you."

***

Looking at herself in the mirror, thinking back over that night in Miami, Monique thought, *It was like before with Keith. Just like the first time we met. He was so genuine, sweet and so sexy.* She pondered for a moment, then her girlish smile turn to sadness.

How can I be with him again? How can I tell him the real reason for my anger? How can I tell him the reason I scratched up his car and broke out his car window? If I tell him, he will never want to touch me again. How can one routine checkup turn into something so horrifying? Damn that Dr. Maxwell, I hope we take him for everything he's worth.

On the other side of town, Keith was thinking, *Wow, what a weekend we had in Miami. I still can't believe I got to hold her in my arms again. The walk on the beach was so bomb. Damn, I love that woman so much. I just can't wrap my head around the whole Jekyll and Hyde thing. One moment we are so connected, so close, and then she just flipped out on me. And for the life of me, I can't figure out what I did or said to cause it. I just want her to know that I love her.*

The phone rings and Angelina struggles to reach to find it.

"Hello."

"Girl," says a voice on the other end, "you still sleeping? It's almost noon."

"Who is this?" asks Angelina.

"It's me, Kiki."

"Oh, hey, girl. What's up?"

"Well, I was going to come take you shopping but I see now that's not going to happen."

He wakes up, leans over and kisses her forehead. "Good morning, baby."

"Angelina, Angelina, who is that?"

"What, Kiki?"

"Girl, don't play dumb with me. You got a man

over there."

"Yeah, girl. I'll be ready in an hour, just be here."

"Okay. And did I tell you Richard is paying for our day?"

"Richard? Who is Richard?"

"The dude from the club in Miami." They laugh.

"All right, I'll see you in a few."

Angelina turns around to the bathroom to watch this tall, six-pack, cut, chiseled, light-skinned god brushing his teeth. *How do I tell my girls I've been kicking it with Jonathan again?*

***

"Yes, this is Myra. Is Dr. Franklin available?"

"She is, Ms. Le'Reaux. Let me inform her that you are on the line."

"Hello, Myra, this is Dr. Franklin."

"Hello, Doctor. I need to come and talk with you right away. The nightmares are coming back again.

"Okay, can you be here by 1pm today? I had a cancelation."

"Yes, I will see you then."

Hanging up the phone, Myra looks at her reflection in the mirror. Shaking her head with tears in her eyes, she tells herself *It's gonna be okay*. She turns, picks up the phone and dials the shop.

"Hello, Cynthia. It's Myra. Yes, I'm okay. I won't be in till later today and I have an appointment with Donna. Can you call her and reschedule? Thanks, girl. See you later."

***

At the knock at the door, Maxwell leans back in his chair and appears to be busy.

"Come in."

In walks Jasmine, 5 feet 8, with an aerobics instructor body, fair-skinned, hazel eyes and long silky hair.

How could someone so beautiful be so evil?

"Hello, Mad Max," she says in a soft enticing voice.

Not looking up from his work, Max says, "Hello, Jasmine. What do you need?"

"Max, I was in town and thought I'd stop by and

say hello. I mean, you left so quickly and didn't even speak at the club."

"Look, Jasmine, I didn't have anything to say then and I don't have anything to say now. So, thanks for stopping by. I need to get back to work."

Walking close to the desk, placing both hands on it and leaning forward to reveal her perfect cleavage, she says, "Oh come on, Max, baby, don't be like that. It's me, your Jazzy."

"No, Jasmine, you're Anthony's girl, wife, whatever. Why are you here and where is your husband?"

"I told you, I came to see you. Anthony is out of town for the weekend."

Looking up from his work, he connects with her eyes. *Damn*, he thought, *she is so beautiful. No, Max, remember the pain.*

Jasmine walks around the desk and reaches to rub his shoulders. Maxwell jumps out of his seat.

"Ooh wee," says Jasmine, "still the same sexy man I fell in love with."

"You mean out of love with, right?

"Okay, I deserve that, but you know you still want me," she says, walking into his personal space.

***

Answering her cell phone, Angelina says, "Hello. Hey, Kiki, I'm on my way down. Jonathan, I'm leaving, I'll be back soon."

"Wait, baby, let me walk you down."

"No, baby, please."

"Angelina, why don't you want anyone to know we are spending time together?"

"Come on, John. You know why; you know the history. I'm just not ready yet. Baby, please."

"Okay, Ange, okay." He kisses her on the lips. "Have fun."

Angelina walks out the door, looking for Kiki's car but sees a limo instead. She smiles and shakes her head.

"Girl," she says as the chauffeur opens the door, "what did you have to put out to… Never mind, I don't even want to know." The door closes and they head off for a day of shopping and fun.

***

"Hello, Myra, come in and have a seat," says Dr. Franklin. "So, on the phone you said that the nightmares are returning. Which ones?"

"Just the last few that I had."

"Do you feel comfortable talking through it, Myra?"

"Yes, Doctor. The dream starts out with me making a phone call to Daryl to come over so we can talk about our relationship. He comes over, we eat, and then the drama starts. The conversation begins with me just explaining to him that it seems that things between us are not going in a positive direction. That I can tell by his actions he is no longer satisfied with what we have, and that he doesn't have to stay with me just for the sake of staying. That I want him to be free to live his life as he wishes, without being tied down when he clearly doesn't want to be. I let him know I will miss him but his happiness and, shoot, my own is important to me.

"And then, without warning, he slaps me so hard across my face that I fly out of my chair and hit my head on the wall. As I struggle to stand to my feet, he grabs me by the throat and slams me on the glass coffee table, which shatters on impact. Leaning over me, he calls me all kinds of bitches and whores, telling me if he can't have me, no man will ever want me. He punches my face repeatedly with his fist. Blood splatters. He picks up a piece of broken glass and begins to slice at my chest and stomach." Pausing to take a deep breath as tears roll down her face, Myra clenches Dr. Franklin's hand.

"Myra, do you want to continue?" ask Dr. Franklin.

She nods and begins again. "He then forces my legs open and jams his fist inside me. I scream in pain as he tells me to shut up or he will kill me. The next thing I'm, waking up in the hospital days later, hearing my son tell an investigator how he came home to find me in a pool of my own blood."

***

Reaching for his office door, Maxwell finds himself trapped between the wall and the unsettling invasion of Jasmine's lips pressed against his.

Pushing her away and wiping his mouth, he says, "What the hell is wrong with you, Jasmine?"

Opening the door he guides her out the door with his hands. "You need to leave and you need to leave now."

Glancing back at him with a glare in her eyes, she says, "Okay, Mad Max. I will go but this is not the last time I will see you. Just remember this, boo boo. I may have lost you but no one else will ever be able to fully have you because you are still in love with me."

"You are crazy. I can't believe you think I'm still in love with you. Despise you, feel sorry for you. But love you? Sweetheart, you got me completely confused with some guy who gives a damn. Jasmine, do not *ever* come to my job again! Leave me the hell alone. Oh, and tell my brother I said hello and that he should keep his dog on the leash," as he slams the door.

***

"So girly, where do you want to stop first?"

"What?"

"And why you looking at me like that?"

"Come on, Kiki. What are you doing? This is getting out of hand."

"Angelina, what are you talking about? I'm just a

single girl out here enjoying herself. If I was a dude, everyone would be calling me the man. Because I'm a chick, I have to be a hoe or worse. Is that what you're saying?"

"No, Kiki. I'm worried about you. Why are you doing this? This is not you and you know it. Ever since your incident with Cameron, you have just been reckless. Reckless with your heart, with your emotions, and your body. And don't tell me you didn't have to put out to get all this."

"Ange, can we not do this right now and just enjoy the moment? Please."

"All right, KiKi, but this conversation isn't over."

As they look out their windows, Kiki flashes back in her mind to the moment she first met Cameron Phillips.

Cameron Jermaine Phillips II, with his fine behind, a tall, light-skinned, big, solid, heavyset brother with long eyelashes. And them damn eyes! When the sun hit them, it looked like speckles of gold had dropped in his eyes; and talk about smelling good.

Ooh wee Jesus, anything that man wore just did

something to me. We first met over the telephone, we had a cool conversation. I remember him saying it was late and he needed sleep cause he had to be up early to go to work. I really didn't want the conversation to stop so, before I knew what was coming out of my mouth, I told him he should come by. I didn't think he'd really come but he called my bluff. The next thing I knew he was knocking on my door. We talked, we cuddled, it was so amazing. The next week at work, I was minding my business, doing what I do when someone walked up behind me, touched me in the small of my back, and said "Hello, gorgeous."

I stopped, froze and slowly turn my head to the left. It was Cameron, he just stopped by to say hi. From that moment on, it was like a whirlwind romance. He was at my house every night for dinner, hanging out with me, watching movies, kicking back, laughing, just having a good time. Before I knew it, he had the key to my apartment. Then the next thing I knew, we were pretty much living together. Things were going so well. I used to love how we would sit in his Durango, listening to music and talking for hours.

I wanted to do something special for his birthday so I created what I call a 12 days of birthdays. Basically every day, for 12 days up until his birthday, which is the 12th of this month, I would make sure he got a special gift and a special note. I went so far as to plan a boys' night out for a surprise by contacting all his friends.

Everything was so well planned. And then something changed. All of a sudden he didn't come over as much or call as much. I thought, " *He's tired. He works a really tough job and probably just needed to rest"*, which was no problem. I really didn't trip. And then, as they say, the shit the fan.

We had just got off the phone. He was sharing about the things that made me so beautiful and attractive to him: how strong I was, a motivating force I was in his life and things like that. About an hour later, I get a text from my girl, telling me to call her. I called her and she dropped the bomb on me that he's cheating on me. I asked, "How would you know?

She said, "Because I'm looking him right in his face!" Wow, talk about devastated! Talk about hurt, destroyed, confused. How many emotions were running through me at that moment?

So, I leave the event I'm at, get home and all I wanna do is find some way to hurt him, call somebody to hurt him. But all I could hear was the voice of my pastor preaching about grace and forgiveness. Who'd a thought my life would be the example of that Sunday's sermon?

So I did the only thing I knew how to do at that moment; I just prayed.

After a few days of crying my eyes out and having a hard time, I got myself together, picked up the phone and called Cameron. I told him he needed to come get his stuff and bring me back my keys. Of course, he tried everything he possibly could to get out of having to see me face to face. He even said to leave his stuff outside the door and he would just slide the keys under the door and we'd be good. I told him, "If you were man enough to do what you did, you should be man enough to look me in my face".

So later that afternoon, he comes over and lets himself in. I told him, "I'm in the room".

He comes to the room, head hung down, sunglasses on so he doesn't have to look me right in the eye or should I say so I can't look him in the eye. I asked him why.

Was I so bad that he had to go sleep with another woman?

Was I not giving him what he needed?

Do you know he gave me the bullshit answer that I was pushing him in a direction he didn't want to go. Negro, please!

Nobody had a damn gun to his head, pushing him in the wrong direction. I said I'm a good woman and you've never experienced that before. I mean if taking the last of what I have to throw a birthday party for your son because things were really financially strapped for you, because I love you; If that's pushing you in the wrong direction then excuse me for being a good woman.

If supporting you and being there for you when your family was turning their back on you and friends weren't there for you, making sure you had a place to lay your head every night, a good meal in your stomach every night, lunch every day when you went to work; if that was pushing you in a direction you didn't want to go in, again, excuse me for being a good woman.

So I said "Can I get a better answer than some bullshit?"

He looked at me and said, "Okay, it was just me. I can't explain it. I just got greedy."

I said, "And got your ass busted." I kinda chuckled, shook my head, said "Whatever."

I handed him his stuff, took back my keys, and told him when he felt like he could be a man and come clean, to let me know. I pointed and said, "You know your way out."

A few weeks went by and it was strange! Our conversation got better: it was crazy! And before long, you guessed it, we were back together.

I gave him the benefit of the doubt because we all make mistakes, we all do things that are unforgivable. I kept thinking how God forgives me when I do worse than what he did so I decided, one more try. Things were going great once again. And then, train wreck.

He calls me one day and says, "I think I need to be alone and be single so I can develop some things on my own. I feel that I can't really give you what you need."

Really? With all we've been through this year and a half, you don't think you can give me what I need?

So yes, I've been devastated ever since and yes, I'm a little reckless. I'm a little out there but tell me, who wouldn't be? Right now it's the only way I know how to deal with the pain. Ange doesn't know the true whole story; she's going by what she sees. Maybe someday soon I'll explain it to her. But for now, I'm going to enjoy doing me.

***

Back at Le'Reaux's, it's business as usual. The shop is packed at 3 p.m. in the afternoon when Myra arrives from her appointment with Dr. Franklin.

"Hey Cynthia, I'm here, girl. Thanks for holding it down for me. You are awesome."

"No problem, really. Are you okay?"

"Yeah, I'm fine. So what do I have next?"

"Well, a new client will be here at 4 p.m. His name is Maxwell, he's coming in for a cut."

"Well, why didn't you or James take him?"

"He specifically asked for you."

"Really? Hmm. Well, I guess I will just have to wait and see." A few minutes later, her boys come in to the shop. Nathan runs and jumps in his mom's arms.

"Hey, my baby, how was school?"

"Good, Mama," as she leans to give Immanuel a kiss on the cheek.

"Thanks for picking up your brother for me."

"No problem, Mom. Are you all right?"

"Yes, baby, I'm good. I left the roast in the oven on low so it should be done, and the potatoes and green beans are on the stove."

"Okay, Mom. What time will you be home?"

"I should be there around six." Giving her kings a hug, she says, "Be careful crossing the street and, Nathan you listen and mind your Bo Bo."

"Okay," Nathan replies as they walk out the door. Myra heads to the back office to sit down for a moment to breathe. She hears a knock on the door.

***

Max is sitting at lunch with Keith. "Max, did you make the call?"

"Yeah, man, I made an appointment for 4 p.m. To

get my haircut. I said I wanted her specifically."

"Okay, player, I'll see you."

"Whatever, man. Make sure you tell Monique I said thank you."

"Yeah, when I see her."

"Keith, you know you're trying to figure out how to see her tonight."

"Well Max, maybe if you can score up an outing with Ms. Le'Reaux, we could double and then I can see her."

"Always gotta be something in it for you."

"Well, I might as well get something out of it after what I had to put myself through to find out who she was."

"Oh, like that was so painful for you." Looking at his watch, Max says, "I better get back to the office to finish up. Almost time to head to Le'Reaux's."

***

"Yes."

"Your 4 p.m. is here, Myra."

"Okay, I'll be right out. Please have him washed

and prepped."

"Okay, girl. He is fine."

Myra freshens up and then heads out to her area. She is standing with her back to the door and getting her tools ready when Max walks over. "Is this where I sit?" he says.

Without looking up, she says, "Yes."

"Thank you, Queen," Max responds, grabbing her attention.

As she slowly looks up in the mirror to see the man from dinner and the club a few weeks ago, Myra almost loses her breath.

"You're welcome," stumbles out of her mouth. Max takes a seat in the chair.

***

A few weeks later, the four of them are sitting at the table at the Ruth's Chris Steak House, laughing and enjoying each other's company.

"So, Myra, tell me again how Mr. Smooth introduced himself to you."

"Well, as you know, he came to the shop and was my 4 p.m. appointment a few weeks ago. He introduced himself as Max, a friend of Keith's. I asked him why he'd asked for me and not one of my super talented barbers. He replied-"

Max interrupts. "I only wanted to be touched by the hands of a queen."

Myra elbows Max in the side and laughs. "Anyway, he began to allude to the fact that he had seen me the weekend we girls were out on the town a while back. You remember, Monique, the night you and Keith got reacquainted."

"Oh yeah," says Monique. "As he was leaving-"

Max interrupts again. "I said," clearing his throat, "and I quote, 'Thank you for using your gifted hands to give me such a clean shave and cut, my queen.' As I watched her walk to the counter to make my payment, I knew this was my only chance and I had better make good on it. So I looked her in the eyes and said that I would not accept no for an answer; a yes from her was the only acceptable response. Her big beautiful eyes widened as I continue to tell her that I was taking her to dinner Friday, December 2nd at 7 p.m.

She opened her mouth and said, 'Well, Mr.

Anderson, can a woman at least get a phone call or two before the date?' and handed me her card with her number on it."

"Damn! You rock, girl. I thought Max had the corner on being smooth. Looks like he may have met his match," Keith explained.

***

Back at Angelina's, the fireplace is lit and soft, jazz is playing in the background and two chilled wine glasses with a bottle of Cristal sitting on the table. The doorbell rings.

"Just a moment," Angelina calls as she approaches the door. Opening the door, she is greeted with Jonathan's warm smile and a bouquet of roses.

"Come in, baby."

As he steps inside, she gives him a warm embrace. *Damn, he is so sexy. I love the way this man smells.* She leads him to the white, plush, bearskin rug in front of the fireplace.

Jonathan reaches for the glasses and the bottle of Cristal and pours them a glass. "Baby, do you remember the night we got reacquainted?"

"How can I forget that night?" says Angelina. "It was the night we all ended up at the same club in Miami. I was on the dance floor and I kept feeling like someone was staring at me. When I finally turned around, I connected with your eyes, like, for a brief moment. Later that night I was sitting at the bar talking to this guy and right when he pulled out his phone to give me his number, you reached across the aisle and gently squeezed my wrist. A chill I will never forget went straight up my spine."

Jonathan laughs.

"What's so funny, baby?"

"Nothing. I was just thinking about what happened on the dance floor."

She smiles. "You mean when I was walking off the dance floor and you gently grabbed my hand and told me I couldn't leave yet?"

"No, sweetheart. When I told you I was going to kidnap you for the night. Before you knew what came out of your mouth you said okay. The look of shock on your face was priceless."

"Shut up. I know I looked retarded." They laugh. "I remember how you told me you weren't trying to get me in bed because you could have been with anyone if that was all you wanted, but that you just did not want the night to end and you just wanted to make the moment last. I remember as we were driving in the car, I kept saying to myself, 'tell him never mind and to take you home,' but I just couldn't get the words out. And then we got to your place. It was so manly but sexy, I 'specially liked the kitchen. We walked in and you gave me the grand tour.

"A little later I asked if it was possible if I could take a shower because I hate being all sticky from dancing all night. You told me yes and led me up the stairs to the bathroom then laid out a towel and washcloth, soap, lotion, the works. I thought, 'wow he's done this for before.' I went in, undressed and got in the shower. It was so hot. It felt so good on my body. You came in and peeked at my silhouette as you left the robe for me. I got out, dried off and lotion up, put on the t-shirt and the robe and came out. I stood at the top of the stairs looking over the rail. y

You looked up at me and took a deep breath. I asked you what was wrong. You told me that no woman, nor your sons, had been in that robe and how beautiful I looked. That I looked like a beautiful goddess. I smiled, came down the stairs and sat next to you.

"We talked about so much until eventually I was lying between your legs with my head on your chest, listening to your heartbeat. And then the conversation went from casual to intimate… not sexual but intimate. You began to get inside my head and without you even touching me in any inappropriate way, my body reacted. That was one of the most powerful explosive experiences I have ever had. It was like out of a scene from *Waiting to Exhale*. We lay in your bed in each other's arms all night."

"Wow, you do remember, baby." They click the glasses together and say cheers.

***

It's 11 p.m. My girls are out and I am bored as hell. She picks up the phone and dials into the chat line to record her greeting.

"Hello, this is Kiki. I am 5 feet 4, caramel

complexion, single, brown eyes, dimples, short hair and I can't sleep. Anyone out there who can give me something good to dream about tonight?"

About five minutes later, a message comes through and says, "Hello, Kiki. I understand that you can't sleep and you're looking for a dream. Well, tell me what makes a good dream for you and I'll see what I can do to help create one. I am 5 feet 7, basketball-built, bald head, goatee and hazel eyes. Thomas."

She replies, "Hello, Thomas, a good dream for me can be something full of fun and laughter, like being a kid on a roller coaster, or something wishful like romance or something intimate like a first date." Her phone notifies her there is a message from Thomas.

"Well, miss lady, is it possible to exchange numbers, I hope, and talk about this dream of yours? My number is 404-588-5445. Let me know."

She responds, "Yes, Thomas, my number is 404-556-9845 and I will be waiting for your call." Five minutes later the phone rings. She answers. "Hello."

"Yes, may I speak with Kiki? This is Thomas."

"This is Kiki nice to meet you."

"Before we get to the dream, tell me about Kiki." They go back and forth for about an hour, filling each other in on little details about who they are.

"Well, Thomas, I work as a graphics designer for a magazine firm. Never been married and no children."

"Okay, Kiki, well I have never been married either. I have no children and I am a chef."

Finally Kiki asked Thomas for a picture; he sends one to her phone and she sends one in return. When they see each other, they're startled to realize they have met before. "Wow," Kiki says, "you were at the club that night, weren't you?"

"Yes, I was. I thought you were sexy then and I think you are still sexy now."

She blushes. "Thank you."

"So, about this dream, I'll start it and you add to it. Is that okay?"

"Okay," she says.

"I call you while I'm at work to tell you I can't stop thinking about you and I ask you how your day is going. I ask you if you are still able to accompany me to the black-tie affair I mentioned to you on the phone the night before. You tell me yes and a warm smile comes across my face. I let you know that I will pick you up at 7:30 sharp. We share a few more sweet words between us and I say goodbye and see you soon."

"Well, from there I get to Le'Reaux's about 2 p.m. the day for my full spa appointment. I get my nails and feet done, a full body wrap, a massage, a facial and my hair and makeup done. I get home around 5 p.m. I don't even have to shower because I had the steam bath as part of my treatment. I turn on some music, pour myself a glass of wine, go to my closet and pull out my dress and shoes for the night. I finish getting dressed and await your arrival."

"Nice. Well, I get to the door and knock. The door opens and there in front of me stands a vision of perfection. You look so yummy I can hardly contain myself. We walk to the car, I open the door and you slide in so gracefully. We head to the event. Kiki, are you there?" Hearing her gentle breathing on the line, he realizes that she has fallen asleep. "Goodnight, beautiful. We'll continue another time," and he hangs up the phone.

***

In the car headed home after a wonderful dinner, Myra is looking out the window in deep thought. "Myra, Myra, are you okay, baby?" asks Maxwell.

Coming to herself, she says, "What? Oh yes, I'm fine."

"Can I ask where your thoughts took you?"

"Nowhere really, I mean I was just thinking, well, see, nothing."

"Baby, come on, you can tell me what's on your mind. Just talk to me."

"Maxwell, can I ask you a question?"

"Yes, sweetheart, what is it?"

"Before I ask, I need you to understand that your answer means a lot and I need you to be completely honest with me. I want you to answer for you, not because you think it's what I want to hear."

"Okay, baby. What is it?"

"Maxwell, what are your core values?"

Maxwell smiles at her and answers immediately. "My core values, as you put it, love, is my relationship with God, having stability, family and friends."

Wow, Myra thinks, *this is the first time I didn't get a 'huh?' or 'what are you talking about?' There could really be something to this man.* She smiles back at him.

"Is that what was troubling your mind, baby girl?"

"Well, we've talked over the phone, had our first date but really, what do we know about each other? I mean, is it too soon to make a request like this, Max?"

"Myra, I have wanted to go deeper in our conversations but I didn't want to overstep any boundaries with you."

"Really?" says Myra. "And here I've been thinking the same thing." They look at each other and crack up.

Coming to a red light, Max stops the car and grabs her hand.

"Sweetheart, listen, I want to know everything about you. What brings you joy, what makes you sad, what frightens you, what gives you strength. I want to know, understand and appreciate your core values. Those things that make you who you are. Myra, if you're wondering if I'm interested. I am. If you're wondering if

I want to be serious with you. I do."

Driving into her driveway, he parks the car.

"And if you want to know if this is about getting you in bed, baby, be assured it's not. Myra, I don't want to date you," her eyes widen with confusion. "I want to court you."

"Court me? Wow. I don't even know what to say."

"You don't need to say anything. Let me walk you to your door. Listen, you are a queen. A man who can't value or appreciate that, well, he's not a man."

"Maxwell, I-."

"Don't say a thing." He kisses her on the forehead and nose and then her cheek. "I'll call you when I get home." Myra stares as she watches Maxwell drive off.

***

"Good morning, this is Monique Johnson. Is Keith available?"

"Yes, Ms. Johnson, I will transfer you now."

"Hello, this is Keith Bryant speaking."

"Hello, Keith, this is Monique."

"Hey baby girl, how are you?"

"I'm okay. A little under the weather but okay."

"Do you need anything? Anything I can do for you?"

"No, I'll be fine. Keith, I was calling to see if you and I can get together sometime within the next week. I really need to talk to you about a few things."

"Okay, baby, is everything okay?"

"Yes, Keith. I just feel like I owe you a complete and honest explanation of why things went so wrong between us. Spending time with you these last few months has made me realize that you deserve at least that, if not more."

"Okay, Monique, why don't we get together next Thursday afternoon, say, 2 p.m?"

"That works great for me, Keith. I will call you when I get back into town next week."

"Okay, baby. Be safe and tell your sisters I said hello."

"I will, baby. Talk to you soon." Monique hangs up the phone with tears in her eyes as her twin sisters Tristan and Tori hug her.

***

"So, miss lady, how are you enjoying the salmon?"

"It's tasty," Kiki responds, looking across the table at Thomas.

He smiles back at her. "I must say getting to know you these past few months has been quite enjoyable. There is so much to you."

"What do you mean, so much to me?" asks Kiki.

"Well, love, I mean you are so complex, but in a very sexy, intriguing way. You're nothing like the materialistic, self-centered woman you try to portray."

"Ah, really? That's how you see me, Thomas?"

"No, baby, that's what you want people to believe. That you are this cold, heartless person and you're not. Kiki, baby, why do you do this?"

"I don't know how else to protect myself from being hurt ever again by another man. Thomas, I have a hard time trusting and that's why, even though we have such a great time when we are together, I don't think I can take this any further than where it is now."

"Kiki, if you would just give me a chance, I can

show you how to trust again." Reaching across the table to grab her hands, he continues. "Baby, I want to be your best friend."

"Thomas, believe me when I tell you it will not work. I am broken and not even God himself can fix me right now. You are better off finding someone else."

"Kiki, I don't want anyone else. I want you, broken and all."

"No, Thomas! Stop it! Don't lie to me. What man wants a broken woman? Really? What is it that you really want, Cameron, to suck me in only to cheat on me with another woman again?"

"Cameron? Baby, who is Cameron?"

Embarrassed by what had just come out of her mouth, Kiki gets up and runs out of the restaurant.

***

"Mama, we're all packed and ready to go."

Myra turns around to see her boys standing in the hallway. "Okay, my kings, let's load the car and head to the airport."

The doorbell rings, and Immanuel answers the

door. "Hey, Max man, what's up?"

"I just had to come by and see the fellas before they leave."

"Mom, it's Max."

Myra comes to the door. "Hey, baby, what a surprise."

"Well, I couldn't let the boys leave without saying goodbye to them. So, Nathan, you ready for this trip?"

"Yes, I can't wait to see my papa."

"Well, I know you're going to have a blast. Here, this is for you." Max hands him a gift card. "Now don't spend it all in one place, okay." Nathan jumps in his arms and gives him a big hug. "Immanuel, this is for you."

"Thanks," Immanuel says and shakes his hand.

"Here, let me help put these bags in the car." Max and the fellas load the car while Myra watches from the doorway. *God, that man is something else.*

"Okay, Mama, all set." Myra closes the door behind her as Max opens the car door for her then kisses her on the cheek.

"Call me later, baby."

"I will," she says. "Everybody, buckle up."

"Yes, Momma," the boys reply. "Mama, I really like Max. He is good to you. Promise me you will spend some time together building a relationship while we are out of the way."

"Yeah, Mama, he would make a great daddy."

"Nathan, where did that come from?" They laugh. "I promise," says Myra.

***

Here we go again. I knew I should have never let him back into my heart. I just don't understand why he keeps doing this to me. I've been there for him over and over and over again. Granted, some of his disappearing acts were not of his own doing. Like the two times he ended up in the hospital, once for being jumped by his baby's mama's psycho boyfriend and the other time for being shot while standing in the kitchen of his house by a stray bullet. But this spending time with me and vanishing for two weeks at a time, I can't do this anymore. I just don't know how to shake this man.

She picks up the phone. "Hello, Jonathan, what

do you want? No, I'm busy and no, I don't have any free time for you the next few days. Yeah, yeah, sure. That's what you always say and the shit just doesn't change. No, Jonathan I.. goodbye."

Angelina hangs up the phone, and falls back on the couch again to cry. She comes to herself about 20 minutes later when there is a knock on the door. She opens it to find Kiki at the door.

"Angelina, girl, what's wrong? Sugar, why you been crying?"

"Kiki, I'm so stupid. I've been seeing Jonathan again."

"Angelina, why are you messing with him again?"

"I don't know, Kiki. I just can't seem to break free from him."

"So what happened this time or do I even need to ask?"

"He did his disappearing act again."

"Damn, girl, you have got to let him go."

"I know but I don't know how to."

"Listen, girl, I got you and we will get through

this together, okay? Come on, let's go get you freshened up cause you look a hot mess."

***

"Good afternoon, Le'Reaux's. How can I help you? Oh yes, she is, just a moment. Myra, your son is on the line." Myra picks up the phone.

"Hello, Mama."

"Hey, baby. How was the flight?"

"It was good and Nathan was a big boy."

"Good, and how were your ears?"

"They hurt a little but I'm okay."

"How's your papa?"

"He's good and you know, Nathan talked his ears off. That's my walkie talkie. Mama, Papa wants to talk to you."

"Okay."

"Hello, princess."

"Hey, Daddy. How are you?"

"I'm great now that I have my boys with me. Who is this Max Nathan can't stop talking about?"

"OMG, that little boy of mine. He is a friend, Daddy, someone I'm getting to know."

"From the sounds of things, he sounds like a good one."

"Dad! Anyways, I got a client coming in. I will call the boys tonight, okay?"

"Okay, princess, be good."

"Okay, Dad. Bye."

Looking down at her phone, she sees she has received a text message from Max. 'I'll see you at seven. Love you, baby.' She smiles and goes back to work.

It's six o'clock finally. Home to shower. Looking at the clock, she thinks, *Not much time, he'll be here at seven. Let's see what's in this closet to put on.*

Myra pulls out some black pants, black boots and a gold and black top. *Sure glad I got my hair braided. At least I don't have to worry about that.*

She heads back to the bathroom, puts her makeup on, comes out and gets dressed, looking at the time: 6:45. *Ooh. So glad I'm ready cause he's always on time.* And right at 7 o'clock on the dot, the doorbell rings.

"Just a minute," she says as she heads for the door.

Opening the door, she sees Maxwell standing

there with the most beautiful bouquet of red roses she's ever seen.

"Well, don't you look cute this evening, miss lady?"

"Thank you, honey. Come on in, I just finished up. Let me grab my coat and I'll be ready to go, okay?"

"Take your time, boo. Do you have a vase I can put your roses in?"

"Sure, just look under the sink in the kitchen." Maxwell goes to the kitchen, gets the vase, fills it with water, places the roses in it and takes it into the living room where he sets it on the coffee table.

"Okay, hun, I'm ready. Let's go."

Getting into the car, Myra says, "So, Maxwell, where are you taking me?"

"Well, we're going to go to a wine tasting event tonight."

"Oh wow, that's different. Sounds like fun."

"Well, I'm sure it will be considering they have a question box."

"What's a question box?" asks Myra.

"Well, pretty much everyone puts a question in

the box. They pull a question, read it and everybody gets a chance to answer."

"A question box at a wine tasting! This should be interesting," Myra chuckles.

Finally at the destination, Max gets out the car, walks around to the other side and opens the door for Myra . "Well, are you ready for a different night, babe?" Maxwell asks.

"Yes, I am. Like I said, this should be interesting."

They head inside and find other couples already there. Sitting at the table, Maxwell introduces Myra to the other couples around the table.

To listen to him introduce me as the woman in his life. Wow, what a feeling. It's been so long since I have felt like this.

As they talk among each other, a box is passed around. Everyone is asked to place a question in the box for later. While Myra is writing her question, "What does love look like to you?" Maxwell is tries to peek, to see what she wrote.

Next, they proceed with the wine tasting, which

is very interesting and a lot of fun. They try several types of wines – dry, extra dry, rosé and sweet. Myra finds that sweet wines are her favorite.

Once the wine tasting is done, they adjourn to the living room by the fire. It is so cozy. Myra snuggles up close to Maxwell. They pass around cheeses, grapes and strawberries and more wine then out comes the question box. One question is read at a time and then everyone has an opportunity to answer. Myra enjoys just listening to everyone else, including Maxwell.

Finally they are down to the last question in the box. Steve, one of Maxwell's friends, points out the fact that Myra has not given a response to any of the questions, so she is put on the spot and has to answer the last one. She agrees but only after everyone else has answered.

And so the question is read "What is the definition of foreplay"?

Myra chuckles as Maxwell gives her the 'oh no' look. You see, they had a debate about this a few weeks ago and he knows she is very passionate when it comes to this topic. He drops his head and shakes it. So once everyone else has answered, Myra scans the room before answering because she knows her response is going to cause a problem.

She takes a deep breath and says, "All of you are wrong."

She gets what she expected: 'Who does this blank think she is?' looks. She proceeds to say that foreplay has nothing to do with a sexual act, but that great foreplay can lead to amazing sex.

Steve's girlfriend Tanya asks her to explain.

So she explains that, yes, while touching the small of her back, or nibbling on his ear can arouse your lover, it's the psychological aspect that is key. What you say and how you say it. When you can stimulate a person's mind, it opens up a world of wonder.

She shares that in order to do this, however, you have to know how to communicate with each other. By the time she is done just talking about it, you can tell that everyone is going to have a pretty good ending to their night.

The next morning, while sitting in his office reminiscing about the night with Myra, Maxwell's thoughts are interrupted by Kim's voice over the intercom.

"Mr. Anderson you have a call on the line."

" Thank you, Kim."

Picking up the receiver, he says, "Hello, this is Maxwell."

"Hey, bro," says the other voice on the line.

"Anthony?"

"Yeah, bro, it's me. I know I am the last person you would ever want to hear from and I wouldn't bother you if it wasn't important."

"What's going on, Anthony?"

"It's Dad."

"What's wrong with Dad? I just talked to him a few weeks ago."

"He slipped and fell down the stairs last night, or early this morning sometime. I found him this morning. He is still breathing but he's unconscious. I don't know what to do. Can you please come home?"

"Okay, Anthony, calm down. I will be there. Tell the doctors I will be there soon."

He hangs up the phone. Walking out of the office,

he says, "Kim, I need you to book me a flight to Atlanta right away. I'm heading home to pack so call me there to let me know what you got for me."

He knocks on Keith's door.

"Come in. Hey, Max, what's up?"

"I am leaving tonight for Atlanta. Pops is in critical condition."

"Okay, let me know if there is anything I can do."

Heading to the car, Maxwell calls Myra. *Baby, please pick up.* "Hello, Myra, baby, it's me."

Hearing the panic in his voice, she says, "Baby, what's wrong?"

"My dad is in the hospital, unconscious. I'm heading home to pack."

"Baby, I'm on my way. I'll meet you at the house." Myra lets Cynthia know she will be gone for the rest of the day, heads to the car and rushes to Maxwell's house. Arriving at the same time as Max, Myra jumps out the car and runs to put her arms around her man. As she hugs him, he breaks down.

"Max, baby, come on, let's go inside." Once

inside she begins to help him pack.

As puts his shirts in his garment bag, Max grabs her hands and says, "Myra, would you come with me? I need you with me, I can't do this on my own. I'll explain it all to you, baby, just say yes.

Myra smiles gently at him. "Okay, baby, I'll go with you."

***

"Hello. Dad. Yes, Dad, I am fine. I'm just calling to let you know that I am going out of town for a few days. I'm going to Atlanta with Maxwell. His dad is in the hospital in a very critical state. No, Dad, he doesn't know about my nightmares and I don't think this is the time to tell him about it. I pray I don't have one either. Okay, Dad, kiss my boys for me and I will call you when we get settled."

Hanging up the phone, she walks out of the room.

"Okay, baby, you ready?"

"Yes," says Maxwell. "Let's go."

***

"Hello, Kiki."

"Hey, Angelina, how are you?"

"I'm doing. I was wondering if you had some free time today."

"Yeah, girl, I'm free. What's up?"

"Good. Can you be at my house by 2 p.m?"

"Sure. Is everything all right?"

"Yes, things are fine. I just need to talk to you."

"Okay. I will see you at 2."

Angelina hangs up the phone then says, "Okay, Thomas. I can't believe you got me in the middle of this, but I believe you are a good man and that Kiki needs to understand what she is getting ready to throw away for some idiot."

"Thanks, Angelina. I owe you big for this. I truly appreciate this."

"Well, if you want to pay up, answer this question for me. What's up with your... never mind."

"What? With who, Angelina?"

"I, well... damn, okay, I might as well tell you. I've been seeing Jonathan again."

"Angelina, you know he's got issues."

"I know but..."

"Look, I will see what I can find out, okay?"

"Thanks, Thomas."

He picks up his phone and sends a text to Jonathan.

***

"Tristan, come quick. It's Monique."

"Oh, my God, Monique. Monique."

"Tristan, call 911."

" 911, what's your emergency?"

"Yes, this is Tristan Johnson at 609 Gravers Lane. My sister Monique Johnson is vomiting and it's all blood. Please send someone quick."

"The ambulance is on the way. I'm going to stay with you on the phone."

"Tori, what do we do?" Monique reaches for her sister Tori's hand. She grabs it.

"They are on the way, sis. Please hang in there."

Monique whispers, "Keith," and then blacks out. Just then there is a knock on the door. Tristan runs to answer it and lets in the paramedics.

"Can you tell us what happened?" Tristan tells

them they found their sister bent over, throwing up nothing but blood; that she just blacked out, and, that she has Hepatitis C. The paramedics move Tori out of the way to attend to Monique.

She comes to for a brief second, "Keith," and then blacks out again.

"Tristan, she is calling for Keith. Call him now."

***

"Listen, Kimberly, I cannot keep doing this and I have to let her know what's going on. I am in love with her and she deserves better than this. I'm going to lose the best thing that has ever happened to me, if I already haven't. I've got to come clean with her. I just have to. She has been there for me through everything, even the things she has no clue about. It's not fair to her. I know we have this son together and I will always be here for my child, but I don't love you. I know you don't love me either, outside of our child."

"Jonathan, how can you say this to me?"

"Come on, Kimberley. You know we are only together for selfish reasons. You promised me financial support to restart my business if I put up a front for your family that we are married. And for what? So we can be miserable for the rest of our lives? And then, there is my other issue that I need to deal with. Look, Kimberly, I don't care if I lose everything; losing her is worse." Jonathan walks out the door, gets in his car and drives off as Kimberly runs behind him, yelling, "I'll make your life hell."

Picking up the phone, he dials Angelina's number. *Please pick up.*

***

"Baby, thank you so much for coming with me. I need to share something with you before we land in Atlanta."

"What is it, Max? What's got you so troubled? I know it's more than just your dad."

Max smiles. "You know me like that already." Grabbing her hand, he says, "Baby, there is more and I probably should have told you this before we left, but I was afraid you wouldn't come. My brother and his wife are going to be there and…"

"And what, Max?"

"And, well, I was with Jasmine before my brother was."

"What do you mean, Max?"

"She is my ex-fiancé and she…"

"What? Really, Max? Really? So you bring me along for what? To be your new show piece?"

"No, Myra, that's not it."

"Wow, why do you men always do crap like this? Everything is always how you can protect yourself without giving a damn about anyone else or how you use others to get what you need. I knew you were too damn good to be true. I knew the other shoe would fall, and it didn't just fall, it kicked me right in the ass."

"Myra, it's not like that, baby. Look at me."

"What, Max? Look, I'm here now just like you planned, and I will be a support for you because of your dad. But when we get home," she says, pulling her hands from his, "we got some talking to do."

***

"Hello, can I speak to Keith Bryant? It's very

urgent."

"Yes, let me get him on the line. May I ask who is speaking?"

"Yes. This is Tristan, I am Monique's sister."

"Please hold."

"Hello, Tristan, this is Keith. My secretary said that it was urgent that you speak with me. Is everything all right?"

"Keith, it's Monique. She is not doing well."

"What do you mean? What happened?"

"It's too much to explain over the phone, can you get here? I really think you should be here."

"I'm coming to Philadelphia, right?"

"Yes, that's right. The address here is 609 Gravers Lane."

"Okay, I will call you when I land in Philly."

"Okay. And Keith, hurry."

Keith grabs his keys and jacket and heads to his house to get his things together to head to Philly. Dialing Max, he leaves a message explaining what is going on and how to reach him if he needs to.

God, please don't take her from me. Let me get

there, let me see her. I love her so much.

Pulling up at his house, he jumps out the car, runs into the house and up the stairs then packs a small bag, goes out the door to the car and heads off to the airport. Reaching the airport, he calls Tristan to let her know he will be in Philly in a few hours.

"So what happened? I don't understand."

"Keith, I'd rather not tell you over the phone."

"Tristan please, what is it?"

"Keith, my sister has…has…"

"What? Tell me."

"She has Hepatitis C."

"What? My God. How? When?"

"She has been battling it for about a year."

One year, Keith thought. *That's about the time our relationship ended.*

"Tristan, is that why, is it … that's why she broke it off with me, why she got so angry and what she wanted to talk to me about when she got back, isn't it?"

"Yes, Keith, it is."

"My poor baby."

"Keith, are you okay?"

"Yes, I am. I will call you when I land."

Keith hangs up the phone. As he sits on the plane, he keeps reliving the night they ended over and over again in his head. *Why didn't I see it, why didn't I stay?* The flight to Philly seems to take hours. Getting to his rental car, he calls Tristan.

"Hey, Keith, glad you made it. When you get to the house, there will be a gate, the code is 7779311."

"Really, Tristan? 7779311?"

"Sorry, what can I say? I'm a big Prince and The Time fan."

Okay, see you in a few."

Following the directions on the GPS, he arrives at the gate, enters the code and drives up the driveway to the house.

As Keith pulls up to the door, Tristan is waiting for him. Keith gets out the car and walks towards the front door in a hurried pace. "Tristan? Hi, I am Keith."

"Hello, Keith. Please come in."

"You have a beautiful home."

"Thank you. It was left to us when our parents

passed away."

"Oh, your parents are deceased?"

"Yes, they were killed by a drunk driver three years ago."

"I'm sorry."

"Thanks. Well, let me show you to your room so you can put down your things and then we can head straight to the hospital."

"Okay, thank you." Keith goes to the room, freshens up and then comes back down stairs to find Tristan talking to the cook. *Wow*, he thought, *I never knew Monique lived like this. She never really talked about it and I wonder why.*

"Keith, this is Giovanni, our cook and he will make you whatever you like."

"Nice to meet you." They shake hands.

"Well, would you like something to eat before we go or are you ready to go now? Giovanni, can we have Mexican tonight?"

"Sure, I'll get started on it right away. I'll make your favorites."

"Thanks, G. See you later." Keith follows Tristan

to her car, a black and teal Mustang 5.0. "So, Keith, how did you and Monique meet?"

"Straight to the point, aren't we? Well, I was at a fundraiser for one of the hospitals to raise money for children with…"

"Children with what, Keith?"

"Wow, children with hepatitis and your sister was there. I watched her interact with these kids for hours. She was so gentle with them. I mean, just watching her kind of pricked my heart."

"Yeah, that sounds like sissy."

"Anyway, eventually I got up the nerve to approach her. I introduced myself. We pretty much stuck to each other that night, talking about how to help the children. By the end of the night, we had planned our first date. We instantly clicked."

"Wow, Keith, sounds like love at first sight."

"Well, for me it was. Our relationship was growing fast and strong. We shared so many great moments together."

" So tell me, Keith, is my sister a tiger in the bedroom?"

"Tristan!"

"I'm sorry."

"Well, to be honest, we have not... I mean, we didn't have sex. She was very firm on where she stood with that and I respected that value in her. Uh! Yes, and then all of a sudden everything fell apart. I guess I know why now, but then it hurt like hell." Pulling up to the hospital, Keith lets out a big sigh.

"Are you nervous?"

"Yeah, a little. I just don't know how I'm going to feel, seeing her like this." As they enter the hospital and turn the corner to her room, they see Tori standing in the hallway, sobbing.

"Tori, what's wrong?"

Just then the doctor comes out of Monique's room. "Okay, she is settled now."

"Settled now? What do you mean," asks Tristan.

"I had to put your sister in a medically - induced comma due to the severity of the pain she was experiencing, and to avoid an increase in her medication. We are diligently searching for a matching donor. Her liver is failing and if we don't find a match soon, she is not going to make it."

"Do you think it is possible for me to go in and see her?"

"Sure, but you must put on a gown, mask and gloves before going in. Let me show you where the items are." Keith follows the doctor to a room just around the corner.

"Doc, can I ask you a question? I know without your liver you will die but how long can a person last without one"

"Keith, not very long. Why do you ask?"

"Well, I love this woman so much that if I were a match, I would give up my liver so she could live. Her sisters need her. She is all they have. Please don't tell the twins about this conversation, but I do want to see if I am a match."

The doctor leaves, pondering the conversation they just had. Keith walks into the room to see Monique. He takes a deep breath.

***

As the plan touches down in Atlanta, the hot, 98

degree, humidity filled air can't even steam the cold chill between them. As the plan taxies to the gate, Maxwell tries to muster up something to say.

"Myra," he says, "welcome to my home."

She just glances at him from the corner of her eye. The captain turns off the Fasten your Seatbelt sign. Several passengers grab their belongings from the overhead bins and exits the plane. Myra and Max stay seated until the plane is almost empty.

On exiting the plane, Max goes to the car rental counter and takes care of the reservation. They head out to the car. Maxwell opens the passenger door for Myra and closes it. He stands and stares at her through the window for a few moments then proceeds to put the luggage in the trunk.

Getting in on the driver's side, he says, "Myra, baby, please say something. This silence is killing me."

"What do you want me to say, Max? Obviously you have said enough for the both of us. So does your family even know I am coming?"

"Yes, babe, they know you are with me."

"And just what do they know, Max?"

"They know that you are special to me."

"Is that right? How special can I be if you couldn't even tell me what was going on? You make me feel like I'm some kind of friend with benefits, some kind of trophy on display. Or am I just your cover for your feelings concerning Jasmine? Do you still have feelings for this woman, Max? Is that it?"

"No, Myra, I don't have feelings for her." Staring straight ahead, Max thinks to himself, *But maybe I do.*

Pulling up to the house, Myra takes out her little makeup kit to freshen up and hide the tear stains on her face. Max gets out and opens the door for her.

Stepping out the car, she says, "Wow, what a beautiful home."

Grabbing the bags from the trunk, Max reaches for Myra's hand. She pulls it away as they walk to the door.

Just then the door opens and there stands Anthony. "Hey, Max, thank you for coming."

"Yeah, bro, you're welcome. Anthony this is..."

"You must be Myra, welcome to our home."

They walk inside the house and into the living room to

have a seat.

"So, how is Dad doing?"

"Well, right now he is still unresponsive and the machines are helping him breathe."

"So, what happened?"

"We are still not sure, whether he lost his balance and fell down the stairs, or he may have had a heart attack...we should know more today."

"Hello, where is everyone?"

"We are in the living room, baby."

In walks Jasmine. "Hello, Max and..."

"This is Myra," says Max.

Extending her hand, she says, "Hello, Myra, I am Jasmine."

As they shake hands Myra mumbles to herself, "She's beautiful." Glancing at Max, she notices a slight change in the expression on his face.

"Well, let me show you to your room." Jasmine leads them upstairs to the south end of the hall. The French doors open to reveal a room that looks like it came from one of those fancy living magazines.

"I'll leave you two to get settled and to go check

on lunch."

Myra takes her bag from Max and starts to unpack it. "Myra, sweetheart, can we please talk about this?"

"Maxwell, I know that we have not been together long but correct me if I'm wrong. Weren't you the one who said you wanted an exclusive relationship with me? Maybe I need to clarify what 'exclusive' means to me. See, sugar, 'exclusive' means that I am not your buddy, your friend with benefits, your around-the-way girl. I means I am your woman and you are my man. That we support each other, respect each other, keep lines of communication clear and open and that we protect each other. Right now, you have not communicated with me and you have left me uncovered and unprotected. We are supposed to be devoted to one another, without questions. Right now, I am questioning.

"Look, Maxwell Thaddeus Anderson, it was clear to me by the expression on your face when she walked into the room that there are still some unresolved emotions tied up in you. I refuse to be dangled in limbo. When we get back home, I think it will best that you and

I take a reprieve. I think you need time to work through this obvious unresolved issue before this right here, you and I, can go any further."

Myra picks up her bag and opens the door to the adjacent bedroom. "I'm going to take a shower and get cleaned up." She closes the door with tears in her eyes as Maxwell just stares.

Anthony knocks at the door. "Hey, bro, lunch is ready."

"Okay, thanks." Tapping on Myra's door, he says, "Baby, lunch is ready. Are you coming?"

"No, I'm not hungry. I'm going to lie down and rest."

"Okay, I'll be back after I eat."

"Uh hmm. Whatever."

Maxwell heads downstairs, feeling very uncomfortable in the room with just Anthony and Jasmine. "So, when are we going over to hospital to see Dad."

"At about 4pm, that's usually when they have completed monitoring for a while. So how did you and Myra meet? She seems like a nice person."

"We met through some mutual friends."

"She is quite different from the women you usually date."

"Yes, she is, Jasmine, in more ways than one. She is not stuck up, self-centered or high maintenance. And it's beautiful to be in the company of a woman who is just down to earth. Anyway, I think I'm going to take a stroll in the garden and then head upstairs to shower and relax. I'll be ready at four."

"Okay, and Max? Thanks again for being here. I really do appreciate it."

Maxwell nods his head and goes out back to the garden. Catching Jasmine gazing in his direction, Anthony says, "Something outside got your attention, Jasmine?"

"Uh, oh, no, not really."

***

Checking to make sure that everything is set for the game, Angelina is thinking, *I got the beer, the snacks and the surround sound on blast…*when the doorbell rings.

"Just a minute. Hey, Kiki, it's about time you got

here. The game is about to start."

"I know. Sorry for being late. I got caught up with…"

"I already know, girl. I wish you would leave him alone and give… never mind."

"Who, Angelina? Thomas. Is that who you were going to say? Girl, I have left Rich. That's why I am late; I was breaking it off with him. I know I had a good person in Thomas but I am too out of control to be with someone like him. Come on, girl, let's go in the family room and get set for game time."

"Kiki, trust me, things are gonna work out for you, I just know it. And, hum, you are rooting for the Broncos right?"

"You know it, girl! Orange and blue baby, orange and blue."

"Oh, Kiki girl, I invited someone else over to watch the game with us."

"Okay, cool, who is it?"

Just then the doorbell rings.

"Can you grab the door while I get the wings?"

"Okay, girl, I'll get it."

Kiki walks over and opens the door. There, to her surprise, stands Thomas.

"Hello, Kiki."

"Hi, Thomas," she says as she turns quickly and goes to take a seat on the couch, leaving him at the door.

"Hey, Thomas," Angelina yells from the kitchen, "come on in and make yourself comfortable."

Turning in Angelina's direction, Kiki gives her an evil look.

"So Kiki, how have you been?"

"I've been all right, Thomas, and you?

"Okay, I guess."

"Just okay?"

"Yeah, for now anyway. So, what have you been up to? And you look great by the way."

Kiki smirks. *What is he up to? I am not doing this. Keep it together, girl. You are not ready to explore any further possibilities with this man.*

"Well, thank you. I've not been doing much."

"So the game tonight should be good, you think?"

"I 'm sure it will be, Thomas."

"Look, I can't do this, Kiki," he says, moving closer to her. "I need to let you know, honey, I miss you. I miss your smile, your touch, the way you communicate with words, our talks. Baby, I miss you. Listen, I know you went through a hard relationship and I know you don't trust like you used to but I just want to be the one who supports you through this. To be there for you."

"Really, Thomas?"

"Yes, love. I'm not asking you to do anything except giving me the opportunity to show you what a good man is."

"I don't know, Thomas. I'm so messed up in the head and my emotions right now."

"Okay, and why do you have to go through this alone? Baby, let me be there for you. Do I want a relationship with you still? Yes, I do, but like I told you before, just let me start by being your friend. Baby, we still have a dream to finish, remember?" Kiki smiles. Thomas gets up and moves closer to her.

"Now that's what I'm talking about," Angelina says, looking at the two of them. Thomas grabs a plate, fills it with snacks and hands it to Kiki.

"Okay," says Angelina, "here we go. It's kick off time."

***

Please pick up, please pick up.

"Hello, this is Ange."

"Baby, it's Jonathan."

"Who?"

"Jonathan."

"Wow, really? What do you want?"

"Can I talk to you? It's important."

"Hold on. Hey, I need to take this call. I'll be back."

"Is it Jonathan?" Kiki mouths.

Nodding her head yes, she goes into the other room.

"Jonathan, whatever you need to say, hurry up and say it. I'm in the middle of watching the game."

"Angelina, I want to explain to you what's been going on."

"Explain what, Jonathan? That you are in another relationship with another woman? Yeah, I know, I saw you last week, all hugged up with her, with matching wedding bands on, I might add. So there is nothing for you to explain. What I saw was pretty self-explanatory."

"No, baby, wait. I do need to explain because what you saw is not what it is."

Really? That bullshit line? Is that in the "How to Get Over on Your Woman Handbook" given to every man at the age 18?

" Oh really? So why are you calling me from a private number all of a sudden?"

"Baby, look, I really need to talk to you but over the phone just doesn't seem right. Can we meet somewhere?"

"Look, Jonathan, I told you I am in the middle of my game and I have company so if you want to meet, it will have to be later."

"Okay, I'll come over after the game."

"Uh no, we can meet at the cafe down the street. *Every time I get around him, I get weak. No chance of anything happening at the cafe.*

"Okay, call me when the game is over and I'll meet you there."

"Yeah, whatever. Bye Jonathan."

As she walks back into the living room, Kiki asks, "Is everything okay, girl?"

"Yeah, it's all good. He wants to meet and talk."

"About what?"

"Girl, probably some lame ass reason and excuse for what I saw."

"Did you tell him you saw him?"

"Yes, I did. He immediately said it wasn't what it looked like. Typical response. I'm so sick of the "it wasn't me" game."

"Angelina."

"What, Thomas?"

"It's not my place to share my boys' business, but I just caution you to go with a clear head and an open mind and hear him out."

"Thomas, you just trying to stick up for your boy."

"No, Angelina, I'm not."

"So you're telling me he has good reason for what I saw and for his disappearing acts, too?"

"Yes, just hear him out."

"Whoosh! Touchdown!" yells Kiki. "Go,

Broncos, go."

***

After taking a relaxing shower, Maxwell walks over to the bed where Myra is sound asleep. When he reaches down to gently stroke the side of her face, Myra moves away from his touch.

God, how do I fix this? I didn't mean to hurt her.

Hearing a knock at the door, Maxwell walks over to open it.

"Hey, bro, sorry to bother you but the hospital just called. They said we need to come as soon as possible."

"Did they say what was wrong?"

"No, Max, they just said we need to get there."

"Okay. Let me get dressed and I'll be right down."

Closing the door, Maxwell turns around to find Myra up and dressed.

"Baby, what are you doing?"

"Max, I told you I would support you through this tough time with your dad and I meant what I said."

"But, sweetheart, you don't have to get up out of

your sleep to go with me."

"Look, I may be angry with you but I am not so upset that I am blind or stupid. I know

that demon, excuse me, Jasmine, would like nothing more than for me to stay here."

"Baby..."

Placing her hand over Maxwell's mouth, Myra says, "Just get dressed and let's go."

***

"Hello, Jonathan. I'll be at the cafe in five minutes."

"Okay, love, I am already here."

Look, Jonathan, this is it, man, your last chance. Don't blow it, you better get this right.

In walks Angelina. He opens his arms to get a hug. Angelina extends her hand.

Looking hurt, he says, "Hello, sweetheart."

"Hello, Jonathan. So, get to the point. What do you need to say to me? I don't have all night and, please, don't waste my time."

Over walks the waiter. "May I please take your order."

"I'll have a slice of your apple crisp and a cup of coffee."

"Sir, what can I get for you?"

"I'll have the same."

" Okay, I'll get this right out to you."

"Thank you. So, Jonathan, what is it?"

"Baby, listen. I love you so very much and I don't nor did I ever want to hurt you. I know I haven't been right all the time but-"

"Jonathan, stop! Just stop! Here comes the same ole bullshit. I'm done. For once in your trifling life, be honest. I'm not stupid. I knew this was a mistake. I wish you would just be real for once and just talk to me with honesty. I'm leaving."

As Angelina gets up, Jonathan grabs her hand.

"Baby, wait. Please don't leave like this."

"Let go of me, Jonathan. Don't say anything else to me. You are such a …never mind, just leave me the hell alone."

Angelina yanks her hand way and runs out of the cafe in tears.

"Angelina, baby," Jonathan says, dropping his head

in his hands. Then, with a determined look on his face, he gets up to run after her. Reaching the door, he sees her crossing the street and yells her name.

"Angelina."

Angelina stops.

He catches up to her.

"Okay, baby, here's the truth." Just then it begins to rain.

"Promise me you will hear me out."

"Okay, Jonathan. Start with the pictures. Who's the girl?"

Taking a deep breath, he says, "Baby, that is Kim and the little boy is my son. We are not together but I had to make it appear in front of her family that we were together."

She looks at him, disgusted.

"Baby, I know it sounds crazy, but remember when I received the large sum of money for my business?"

"Yes."

"Well, I got it from her and in exchange I had to portray what I was not, her husband. But tonight, before I called you, I told her no more. If I lost everything it didn't even compare to losing you."

She turns her back so he won't see her tears.

He has a child by another woman.

"Baby, I'm sorry but you wanted the truth. Then, three weeks ago, my life fell apart. I had to bury my nephew, who was found dead by his fiancée. And my father found out that my mom is in the beginning of Parkinson's disease. With all that pressure and stress, I fell and fell hard.

"You fell? What do you mean, you fell, Jonathan?"

"Baby, I went on a drug binge."

"Drugs! Jonathan, what?"

"The woman you saw me with was my…"

Just then Angelina's phone rings.

"Hello. Hey Kiki, what's up?"

"Angelina, I just got a call from Keith. Monique is in the hospital in a coma." Angelina looks like she saw a ghost.

"What's wrong, baby?"

"It's Monique. She's in a coma. I've got to go."

***

Walking into the hospital room, Keith loses his composure at seeing Monique lifeless.

My beautiful Nubian Queen.

He pulls up a chair by her side and holds her hand.

Father in heaven, I know it's been a while since you have heard my voice. I ask that you don't hold that against this sweet woman. I am coming to You asking for a miracle. Please give me a chance to love her and her a chance to be loved.

Just then the doctor walks in.

"Keith, I want you to know that you are a perfect match. Are you sure you want to give up your life because that's what you would be doing?"

"Doc, you don't understand. I love her that much."

"Well, consider all the consequences. There is still a chance for a donor to come through."

"Okay, Doc, thank you."

Lord, please make it clear what I should do.

After sitting by her bedside for hours, Tristan

finally comes into the room and finds Keith resting his head on her chest.

"Keith, visiting hours are about over. Are you ready?"

"Yes, I am," he says as he leans over to kiss Monique's forehead. "Baby, I'll be back first thing in the morning."

***

"So what did the doctor say about your dad?"

"We now know that he fell down the stairs due to some kind of fainting spell. Now they are trying to figure out why he fainted. While I was in the room, he actually squeezed my fingers."

"That's a good thing, right?"

"Yeah, but he still has a long way to go."

" I'm going to go to the room. Why don't you go take a shower? You've had a long day."

"Okay."

He kisses Myra on the forehead, grabs his stuff and goes into the restroom.

Shutting the door and turning on the hot shower, Maxwell stares in the mirror. He comes to when

Myra calls through the door that she is going to bed.

"Okay, baby. I'll be out soon."

Maxwell climbs under the hot steaming shower and lets the water beat over him.

This is too much. My dad, Myra. If I had been honest with her from the beginning, I wouldn't be dealing with that stress. I hope Dad comes out of this situation okay.

He slides down the wall of the shower and sobs.

God, I know I have not spoken to You, let alone acknowledged You, since the wedding day. I know You may not even want to listen to me, but I am asking You to touch my father. I don't mean to sound selfish but we need him. And if You can spare a little extra time, can You help me deal with what I've done to my queen? Free me from this emotional curse Jasmine has over me. Why can't we men just talk to our women? We have damaged so many of them just because we don't talk, always trying to be a macho man. God, I am so sorry for hurting her because of my insecurities.

Standing to his feet, Maxwell washes his body and steps out of the shower. Drying off and getting dressed for bed, he hears Myra whimpering in her sleep. Maxwell grabs her arm to shake her gently.

Myra screams out at the top of her lungs, "NOOOOOOO!!!" and swings at Maxwell. He lets her go and steps back.

He calls her name gently.

"Myra."

Myra, not realizing what just happened, wakes up, breathing heavily and looks around dazed.

"Myra, baby, you okay?" He reaches for her.

She grabs his hand and pulls him close and whispers, "He's gonna kill me."

He holds her close and rocks her, asking not a question. At least not for now.

About an hour later, Myra's phone rings.

"Hello? Yes, what? What do you mean she's in a coma."

Oh my God, Kiki, not Monique." Myra just

turns and stares at Maxwell.

Maxwell reaches for his phone to dial Keith.

"Hello?"

"Hey, this is Maxwell. Where are you?"

"I'm in Philly. Didn't you get my message?"

"No, I didn't. Myra just got a call from Kiki that Monique is in a coma."

"Yeah, she is. Max, did you know she had Hepatitis C, man?"

Maxwell, knowing he can't divulge client information, answers Keith with his silence.

"Is that what she has been seeing you about?"

Again he answers that question with his silence.

"Keith, what can we do? No, scratch that. We will be catching a flight tomorrow as soon as we can."

"We?"

"Yes, Myra is with me."

Myra reaches for the phone.

"Let me talk to him. Hello, Keith, hold on, okay?" Myra clicks over and calls Kiki, who calls Angelina, so they are all on the call. They make plans to all be in Philly tomorrow. She clicks back over.

"Keith, we will all be there: me, Kiki, Angelina, Thomas and Jonathan." She looks in Maxwell's direction.

"And Max. Where do we need to go?"

Keith gives her the information and then hangs up. "Max, how are you going to go to Philly with your dad in the hospital?"

"Baby, I'll just fly there in the morning and catch the redeye back. Anthony will understand."

Early the next morning, Myra, Max, Kiki, Thomas, Angelina and Jonathan arrive at the home of Tristan and Tori. They are greeted by Keith, who shows them in and introduces them to the twins. Once settled they gather in the living room.

"Keith, what's going on?"

"Tristan or Tori, do you want to share?"

Tristan begins to fill everyone in on what has transpired over the past few days.

"Hepatitis C?" says Kiki.

"Yes," says Keith. "She has been battling it for about a year now."

"When can we go see her?" asks Angelina.

"Not for a few hours," Tori says. "Would anyone like something to eat? I can have Giovanni prepare something."

"Sure."

Tori heads into the kitchen to talk to Giovanni about preparing a meal for their guests. Tristan takes a moment to show them were they can put their belongings.

Everyone congregates around the table to eat. The silence is so thick you can cut it with a knife. Angelina finally speaks up.

"Keith, how are you holding up? I know, we all know, how much you love her."

"Angelina, this is the hardest thing I have had to deal with in my life. Listen, now that the twins are not in here, I need to tell you something. I found out that I am a perfect match."

"A perfect match for what, Keith?" asks Kiki.

"To be a donor. If we cannot find a donor, I am going to give up my liver for her."

"Keith…"

"I know what that means. But she will live and she has so much more than me to live for."

"Keith, you can't do this. What about the fact that Monique needs you?"

"I know she does and that's why I am willing to be what she needs."

Just then Tori walks back in the dining room. "Lunch is served. As soon as we are done eating, we will take you all over to the hospital." Everyone eats in silence.

To Contact The Author and for Booking

AriQui Books at (276) 6ariqui4

(276) 624-7844

AriQuibooks@gmail.com

www.AriQuiBooks.us

Be On The Look Out For More AriQui Books

Speak To The King In Me

Hear The Queen In Me

Just Talk To Me E-Book & Audio

Left Uncovered (An AriQui Novella Series Vol. 2)

Notes

Movie quote reference: Pretty Hot and Thick taken from the authors favorite movie Phat Girlz.

 1. Phat Girlz is a 2006 comedy film written and directed by Nnegest Likké and starring Mo'Nique. Wikipedia

 2. Initial release: April 7, 2006

 4. Director: Nnegest Likké

 5. Initial DVD release: August 22, 2006

 Song Quote Reference: "777-9311" is the second track and lead single from The Time's second album, What Time Is It?,[1] from The Time album What Time Is It? Recorded for the album at Prince's home studio in May–June 1982, the song was produced, arranged, composed and performed by Prince with Morris Day later adding his lead vocals.

www.ingramcontent.com/pod-product-compliance
Lightning Source LLC
Chambersburg PA
CBHW071143090426
42736CB00012B/2208